PLAYGROUND KINDNESS

Miranda Kelly

CRABTREE
PUBLISHING COMPANY
WWW.CRABTREEBOOKS.COM

Our parents teach us **manners.**

3

They teach us to be helpful and kind.

Good manners help us get along with others.

Use your manners
on the playground.

Thank you!

Take **turns** and be fair.

You're next!

Do your part to keep the playground clean.

Be sure to **share.**

Look out for
each other.

17

Be a **good** sport.

Good game!

Practice playground kindness every day.

Glossary

good sport (GOOD SPORT): A good sport is someone who uses good manners even when they lose.

manners (MAN-urz): When you use good manners, you are acting polite and kind.

share (SHAIR): When you share, you are using something with someone else.

turns (TURNZ): Turns are chances to do something.

Index

School-to-Home Support for Caregivers and Teachers

Crabtree Seedlings books help children grow by letting them practice reading. Here are a few guiding questions to help the reader with building his or her comprehension skills. Possible answers are included.

Before Reading

- What do I think this book is about? **I think this book is about being kind to others. It is about how to get along with others on a playground.**

- What do I want to learn about this topic? **I want to learn about different ways to be kind to others.**

During Reading

- I wonder why... **I wonder why the children on pages 16 and 17 are sad.**

- What have I learned so far? **I have learned that some ways to be kind are to share, take turns, and use manners.**

After Reading

- What details did I learn about this topic? **I learned that good manners teach us how to be helpful and kind. They help us get along with others.**

- Read the book again and look for the vocabulary words. **I see the word _turns_ on page 11 and the word _share_ on page 14. The other vocabulary words are found on pages 22 and 23.**

Library and Archives Canada Cataloging-in-Publication Data

Title: Playground kindness / by Miranda Kelly.
Names: Kelly, Miranda, 1990- author.
Description: Series statement: In my community |
"A Crabtree seedlings book". | Includes index.
Identifiers: Canadiana 20200388150 |
 ISBN 9781427129598 (hardcover) |
 ISBN 9781427129697 (softcover)
Subjects: LCSH: Kindness—Juvenile literature. |
LCSH: Courtesy—Juvenile literature.
Classification: LCC BJ1533.K5 K45 2021 | DDC j177/.7—dc23

Library of Congress Cataloging-in-Publication Data

Names: Kelly, Miranda, 1990- author.
Title: Playground kindness / by Miranda Kelly.
Description: New York, NY : Crabtree Publishing, 2021. | Series: In my community, a Crabtree seedlings book | Includes index.
Identifiers: LCCN 2020050788 |
 ISBN 9781427129598 (hardcover) |
 ISBN   9781427129697 (paperback)
Subjects: LCSH: Playgrounds--Social aspects--Juvenile literature. | Kindness--Juvenile literature. | Etiquette for children and teenagers--Juvenile literature. Classification: LCC GV423 .K45 2021 | DDC 790.06/8--dc23 LC record available at https://lccn.loc.gov/2020050788

Crabtree Publishing Company
www.crabtreebooks.com   1-800-387-7650
e-book ISBN 978-1-947632-82-0
Print book version produced jointly with Crabtree Publishing Company NY, USA

Written by Miranda Kelly
Production coordinator and Prepress technician: Amy Salter
Print coordinator: Katherine Berti

CPC20210813

Published in Canada
Crabtree Publishing
616 Welland Ave.
St. Catharines, ON
L2M 5V6

Published in the United States
Crabtree Publishing
347 Fifth Ave
Suite 1402-145
New York, NY 10016

Published in the United Kingdom
Crabtree Publishing
Maritime House
Basin Road North, Hove
BN41 1WR

Published in Australia
Crabtree Publishing
Unit 3 – 5
Currumbin Court
Capalaba QLD 4157

24